Do Intangible Assets Explain High U.S. Foreign Direct Investment Returns?

Benjamin Bridgman*

Bureau of Economic Analysis

September 23, 2008

Abstract

U.S. investors abroad receive a higher return on their assets than their counterparts that invest in the United States. I examine the degree to which excluding intangible assets from the measurement of foreign direct investment can account for this gap. Using a growth accounting framework, I estimate intangible capital stocks for foreign-owned affiliates and find that including unmeasured capital reduces the gap by up to two thirds. U.S. affiliates abroad hold a relatively large share of their assets as intangible capital since they are taxed at the relatively high U.S. corporate rate and intangible investment is expensed. Accounting for intangibles reduces a similar gap in British FDI returns by nearly half.

---

*I thank Dennis Fixler, Ralph Kozlow, Ellen McGrattan, Obie Whichard, Dan Yorgason and seminar participants at the 2007 APET meetings, 2008 Midwest Macro Meetings, 2nd World Congress on Index Measures and the 2008 North American Summer Meetings of the Econometrics Society for comments and Andrew Miller, Anna Rahkman and Chris Zwicker for research assistance. The views expressed in this paper are solely those of the author and not necessarily those of the U.S. Bureau of Economic Analysis or the U.S. Department of Commerce. Address: Department of Commerce, Bureau of Economic Analysis, Washington, DC 20230. email: Benjamin.Bridgman@bea.gov. Tel. (202) 606-9991. Fax (202) 606-5366.

1 Introduction

Measured U.S. net investment position is negative and has been so for over two decades. However, as shown in Figure 1, U.S. net earnings on foreign-owned assets has been positive despite the fact that the net investment position has been growing more negative over this period.

Figure 1: U.S. Net Investment Position and Net Income on Foreign-Owned Assets, 1976-2006

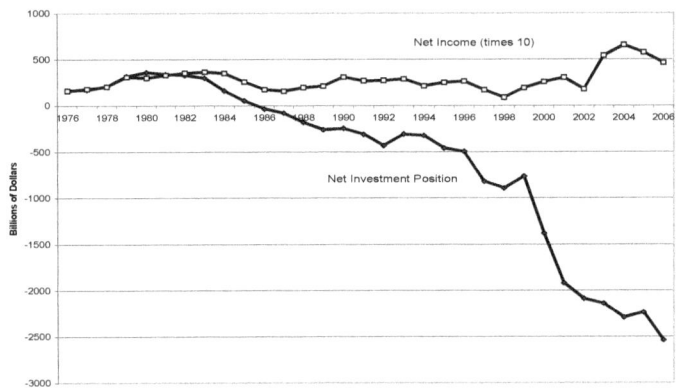

The reason for the continued positive return is that American investors receive higher returns on their investments abroad than their foreign counterparts do on their U.S. investments. The average inward return on foreign assets between 1982 and 2004 was 4.5 percent compared to 5.7 percent for outward investment[1]. American investors also receive higher returns on U.S. investments than foreigners.

The gap in returns is most severe in direct investment. As can be seen from Figure 2, the gap is due to a large gap in returns for FDI. From 1982 to 2004, outward direct investment earned a 7.6 percent return compared to 2.2 for inward FDI. Non-FDI

---

[1]In the paper, "inward" and "outward" are defined from the perspective of the United States.

assets do not show much of a gap, with inward investment earning an average return of 5.2 percent compared to 4.9 for outward investment. The gap in rates of return on foreign investment has been a long standing puzzle. For example, foreign manufacturing firms in the United States have had lower returns than U.S. firms since at least 1951 (Laster & McCauley 1994). In no year do foreign firms have a higher return and the gap has widened with time. Other authors that have analyzed this issue include Landefeld, Lawson & Weinberg (1992), Laster & McCauley (1994), Mataloni (2000), and Hung & Mascaro (2004).

This gap has generated a great deal of interest recently. While returns need not be equal across countries at any given time, the size and persistence of the gap seems quite anomalous. Understanding the nature of the gap is important for analyzing a number of economic issues, such as whether the U.S. current account deficit is sustainable. (See Caballero, Farhi & Gourinchas (2008) and Mendoza, Quadrini & Rios-Rull (2007), among many others.)

Many explanations of this puzzle have been advanced. These include risk compensation, the use of transfer pricing and other methods to avoid taxation (Hines 1999), the use of the dollar as an international standard (Gourinchas & Rey 2006), and provision of liquidity (Caballero et al. 2008), among others. Hausmann & Sturzenegger (2007) suggest that the "dark matter" they use to explain the gap comes from three sources: risk compensation, implicit payment for financial services, and unmeasured intangible capital. This paper explores how much of the gap can be attributed to a novel explanation: differences in intangible asset holdings that result from multinational corporations' (MNC) corporate income taxation.

The National Income and Product Accounts do not include most intangible assets, while they do pick up their returns. Therefore, measured returns are likely to be overstated for countries that invest more in intangible capital relative to those that invest in tangible capital. Portfolio investment captures intangible capital since the price of a share includes the value of its intangible assets (Lev & Sougiannis 1996). Since there is no market price, non-traded firms are valued by a proxy: the purchase price of physical assets adjusted for country specific equity price changes.

The way that MNCs are taxed give an incentive for U.S. based MNCs to hold more

Figure 2: Returns to Foreign Investment, 1982-2006 (Percent)

(a) FDI returns

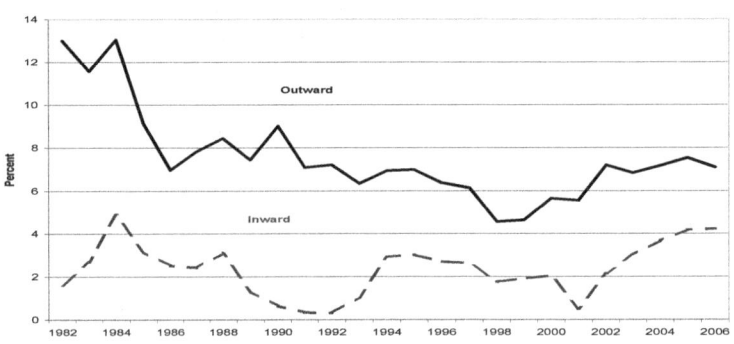

(b) Non-FDI Returns

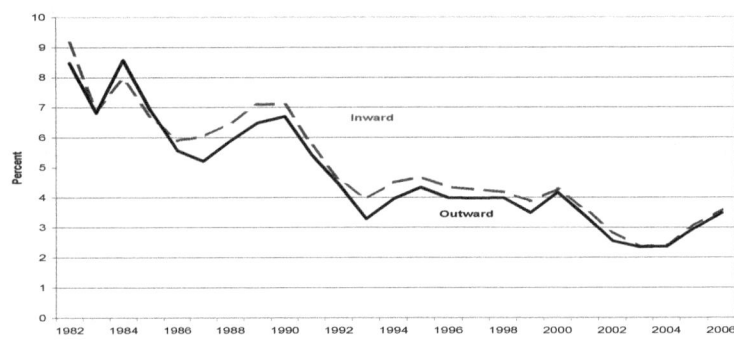

of their assets as intangibles. Since intangible investments are expensed while tangible investments are not, corporate income taxes give an incentive to shift asset holdings into intangibles. The United States has had relatively high corporate income taxes. In addition, the United States taxes the worldwide profits of its MNCs at the U.S. rate, with a credit for payments abroad. Therefore they may be subject to a repatriation tax when profits are returned from lower tax jurisdictions. Since this tax payment is a purely domestic transaction, it is not counted in the balance of payments accounts.

I use a growth accounting framework similar to that used by McGrattan & Prescott (2005) to calculate the contribution of the taxation of MNCs on the returns gap through the accumulation of intangible capital. I assume that after-tax rates of return on tangible and intangible capital are equalized and use corporate income tax rates to estimate the stock of intangible capital held by U.S. direct investors abroad and foreign investors in the United States. The estimates are used to adjust the rates of return on FDI assets.

Accounting for intangible asset holdings reduces the U.S. FDI returns gap by up to three quarters. The average returns gap falls from 4.7 to 1.1 percentage points over the period 1990 to 2001. The overall gap in returns is nearly eliminated when the adjusted FDI rates of return are applied to the overall overseas asset portfolio: The total average annual rate of return is 3.7 percent for foreign owned assets in the United States compared to 3.8 percent for U.S. owned assets abroad. I calculate alternative estimates of intangible assets using R&D expenditures as a proxy for intangible investment and find nearly identical results.

I also apply the model to the United Kingdom. Since 1997, the UK has been in a situation similar to that of the United States: It has a negative international investment position with positive net returns due to higher outward FDI returns. Like the United States, the UK uses worldwide taxation. Including intangible assets reduces the UK's average annual gap in FDI returns from 2.6 percent to 1.5 percent over the period 1997 to 2005, nearly half the gap in FDI asset returns. Adjusting the overall foreign asset returns reduces total gap by half, from 0.53 to 0.26 percentage points.

The results suggest that different holdings of intangible assets as a result of corporate income taxes are a first order cause of the gap in international asset returns. They also underline the importance of accounting for intangible assets in the international investment position. Excluding them have a quantitatively important impact on the measurement of international returns.

This paper is part of a growing literature examining the rates return puzzle, which has been discussed above. Other papers have suggested intangible assets as a source of the returns gap. McGrattan & Prescott (2008) use the returns gap in returns to identify differential openness to foreign investment in a growth accounting framework. Kapicka (2008) uses a similar framework to back out the degree of openness to intangible "technology capital." This paper differs in that it uses taxes to identify intangible asset holdings and estimates intangible assets in the United Kingdom. The impact of openness is discussed below.

Hausmann & Sturzenegger (2007) also examine intangible assets, which they colorfully refer to as "Dark Matter." They revalue assets assuming all assets return a reference rate of 5 percent. This paper only assumes that rates of return are equalized across tangible and intangible assets, rather than imposing a rate of return, and uses independent data on tax rates to identify holdings of intangible assets.

The rest of the paper is organized as follows: Section 2 discusses intangible assets. Section 3 presents the model. Section 4 presents the theoretical results while Section 5 presents the empirical results. Section 6 applies the model to the British case and Section 7 the robustness of the results. Section 8 concludes.

2 Why Intangible Capital?

There are a number of reasons to believe intangible assets may help resolve the returns gap puzzle.

The intangible assets explanation is specific to FDI. Returns to portfolio investment do not show the large gap that direct investment does. When valuing portfolio investment, the market takes into account both tangible and intangible assets owned by the firm. This is not true for direct investment. (By using stock market indices to revalue the book value of assets, BEA methodology will capture changes in the relative holding of intangible assets. However, it will not capture persistent differences in the the relative holding of assets types.)

Omitting intangibles can generate very high rates of return on assets. Multinational companies (MNCs) account for most R&D expenditures, suggesting that omitting intangibles may be particularly distorting to the valuation of foreign-owned affiliates.

There is reason to believe that U.S. MNCs hold more of their assets as intangibles.

Doms & Jensen (1998) find that U.S. MNC's manufacturing plants are more productive (as measured by total factor productivity) and pay higher wages than foreign-owned U.S. plants. This superior performance is consistent with U.S. MNCs holding relatively higher portfolios of intangible assets. Girma, Thompson & Wright (2002) also find that U.S. owned plants in the United Kingdom are the most productive and pay higher wages.

Finally, the United States is not the only country to show a gap. Meissner & Taylor (2006) finds that gaps occur in many countries. As mentioned above, the United Kingdom has developed a situation similar to the United States. Therefore, general explanations are more likely relative to those that are specific to the United States.

2.1   Alternative Explanations

A number of theories have been put forward to explain the gap. I consider each in turn.

Higher rates of return may be a reflection of the higher risk that U.S. investments face. The United States is a mature market and investors looking for higher returns may look abroad (Hausmann & Sturzenegger 2007). Hung & Mascaro (2004) examine whether the countries U.S. MNCs invest in are risky by looking at their bond ratings. They find that the risk gap is small since most investment is in developed countries with similar risk profiles. However, individual projects that they invest in may be riskier.

The return gap may reflect transfer pricing to reduce profits in high tax countries (Hines 1999). While identifying this effect is difficult, attempts to do so have found only minor revenue losses on the order of one percent of tax liabilities (U.S. Deparment of the Treasury Internal Revenue Service 1999, Bernard, Jensen & Schott 2006).

Gourinchas & Rey (2006) suggest that the higher return reflects the "Exorbitant Privilege," a willingness of foreigners to hold dollar denominated assets since the dollar is an important international currency. This theory does not explain why the gap appears in other countries or why it only affects FDI.

A related theory is that the gap reflects unmeasured exports of U.S. financial services that arise from the United States's superior financial depth (Hausmann & Sturzenegger 2007, Caballero et al. 2008). Curcuru, Dvorak & Warnock (2008) find that there is very little gap in portfolio assets once revisions in the data are properly accounted for and that the gap only exists in FDI assets. Forbes (2008) finds evidence in portfolio investment that low income countries accept low returns since they lack developed financial markets. Most FDI investors in the United States are from high income countries. Further, this theory does not explain why foreign investors accept such a large gap in returns in FDI when the gap in portfolio assets is much smaller.

McGrattan & Prescott (2008) also argue that the returns reflect differential investments in intangible capital, but identify the cause as less financial openness in the United States. This paper is similar in that it also identifies intangibles as the source of the gap, though the mechanism for the difference is taxation rather than financial openness. This explanation is discussed in more detail below.

2.2 What are Intangible Assets?

The intangible assets identified in this paper are those that are created and held by the firm. It does not include intangible public capital such as rule of law and political stability. (Such intangible capital figures prominently in World Bank (2006)). While these may affect returns, intangible capital is identified in the model using the incentives of firms to accumulate such capital. There are a number of different such intangible assets. They include patents, trademarks, trade secrets, and knowledge about organizing a firm (organization capital).

Although investment in intangible capital is accepted as a legitimate investment activity by national accountants, it has been generally excluded due to the difficulty in measuring its production and depreciation. The 1993 System of National Accounts (SNA) manual, which contains the basic methodology for computing national accounts for most countries in the world, says of R&D that "[i]n order to classify such activities as investment type it would be necessary to have clear criteria for delineating them from other activities, to be able to identify and classify the assets produced, to be able to value such assets in an economically meaningful way and to know the rate at which they depreciate over time. In practice, it is difficult to meet all these requirements. By convention, therefore, all the outputs produced by research and development ... are treated as being consumed as intermediate inputs even though some of them may bring future benefits."

National accounting is now moving toward including intangible assets in its estimates. The forthcoming SNA 2008 manual will require that investments in R&D be capitalized. Some intangible assets, such as computer software, have already been added to the U.S. national accounts. The United States also produces periodic R&D satellite accounts (Okubo, Robbins, Moylan, Sliker, Schultz & Mataloni 2006), but does not currently incorporate it into the main accounts (Carson, Grimm & Moylan 1994). However, they will be incorporated into the main accounts in the future.

3 Model

3.1 Households

There are I countries, each with a representative household with preferences represented by the utility function:

$$\sum_{t=0}^{\infty} \beta^t u(c^i(t)) \tag{1}$$

where $c^i(t)$ is per capita consumption in country i. Each household is endowed with one unit of labor in each period. The price of consumption in country i is p^i. Lowercase variables refer to per capita quantities while uppercase variables are aggregates. The measure of population in each country N^i grows at the common growth rate γ_N.

3.2 Production

Each country has a representative multinational that has foreign affiliates in all other countries. Output of country $i's$ multinational's affiliate in location j is given by Y_j^i. The parent's output is Y_i^i. (Superscripts refer to ownership and subscripts to location.) Output is produced by a Cobb-Douglas production function:

$$Y_j^i \leq (K_j^{m,i})^{\alpha_m} (K_j^{u,i})^{\alpha_u} (A(t) * N_j^i)^{1-\alpha_m-\alpha_u} \tag{2}$$

where K^m and K^u is tangible (measured) and intangible (unmeasured) capital respectively, N_j^i is labor used and A is labor augmenting technological change. Output can be used for investment or consumption:

$$C_j^i(t) + X_j^{m,i} + X_j^{u,i} \leq Y_j^i \tag{3}$$

The inputs into production, capital and labor, are immobile. Consumption can be costlessly traded to any country. The common productivity trend is given by $A(t) = (1 + \gamma_A)^t$.

The laws of motion for capital are:

$$K_j^{m,i}(t+1) \leq K_j^{m,i}(t)(1 - \delta_m) + X_j^{m,i}(t) \tag{4}$$

and

$$K_j^{u,i}(t+1) \leq K_j^{u,i}(t)(1 - \delta_u) + X_j^{u,i}(t). \tag{5}$$

Labor N in country j is allocated across the local parent and foreign-owned affiliates:

$$N_j(t) = \sum_{i=1}^{I} N_j^i(t) \tag{6}$$

3.3 Taxation

Corporate income of foreign affiliates may be taxed both in the country it is based in and in the parent's home country. The proceeds of each countries taxes are rebated to the domestic household as lump sum transfer $\Psi^i(t)$. Dividends are given by:

$$d^i(t) = \sum_j p_j(t)\{Y_j^i(t) - X_j^{u,i}(t) - X_j^{m,i}(t) - w_j(t)N_j^i(t) - (\tau_j + \tau_j^{i,f})\pi_j^i\} \tag{7}$$

where τ_j is the government in country j's corporate income tax on firms in j, $\tau_j^{i,f}$ is the corporate income tax on foreign profits of affiliate in country j of country $i's$ MNC and

$$\pi_j^i = Y_j^i(t) - \delta_m K_j^{m,i}(t) - X_j^{u,i}(t) - w_j(t)N_j^i(t) \tag{8}$$

The government maintains budget balance in each period, so its budget constraint is given by:

$$\Psi^i(t) \leq \sum_{j=1}^{I} \{p_i(t)(\tau_i \pi_i^j) + p_j(t)(\tau_j^{i,f} \pi_j^i)\} \tag{9}$$

Each household i faces the budget constraint:

$$\sum_{t=0}^{\infty} p_i(t)c^i(t) \leq \sum_{t=0}^{\infty} p_i(t)\{d^i(t) + w_i(t) + \Psi^i(t)\} \tag{10}$$

10

3.4 Equilibrium

The representative household in country i's problem is to maximize utility (equation 1) subject to the budget constraint (equation 10). The representative multinational's problem is to maximize $\sum_{t=0}^{\infty} d^i(t)$, where $d^i(t)$ is given by equation 7, subject to the laws of motion on capital (equations 5 and 4).

The definition of equilibrium is standard.

Definition 3.1. *An equilibrium is sequences of prices $\{p_j(t), w_j(t)\}$ and quantities $\{Y_j^i(t), C_j^i(t), K_j^{m,i}(t), K_j^{u,i}(t), X_j^{m,i}(t), x_j^{u,i}(t), d_j(t), N_j^i(t)\}$ such that*

1. *Households choose $\{\frac{C^i}{N_i}\}$ to solve their problem,*

2. *Firms choose $\{X_j^{m,i}(t), X_j^{u,i}(t), d_j(t), N_j^i(t)\}$ to solve their problem,*

3. *Allocations are feasible.*

4 Model Results

This section presents the theoretical results of the model.

The first implication of the model is that high rates of corporate income taxes increase the incentive to hold intangible assets. Since investment in intangible capital can be expensed, investment in intangible assets reduce the tax burden. Higher taxes reduce the marginal cost of this investment. From the solution to the firm's problem, we have:

$$1 - \tau_j - \tau_j^{i,f} = \frac{\frac{\alpha_u Y_j^i}{K_j^{u,i}} - \delta_u}{\frac{\alpha_m Y_j^i}{K_j^{m,i}} - \delta_m} \tag{11}$$

With higher taxes, the firm sets the marginal product of intangible capital lower relative to that of tangible capital implying that K^u is higher relative to K^m. Worldwide taxes effectively make the tax rates faced by an MNC the maximum of the foreign and domestic rates. Countries with high corporate tax rates and worldwide taxation are likely to hold more of their assets as intangibles. (In effect, high corporate income taxes act as a spur to R&D!) The United States has been on the high end of corporate tax rates, so it is more likely to hold intangible assets.

11

4.1 Taxes and Returns

There are two basic systems for taxing corporate income of multinationals: territorial and worldwide. Under territorial taxation, foreign subsidiaries pay the taxes of country they are located in and do not have any additional tax burden in the parent country.

Worldwide taxation treats the entire MNC as a unified company that faces taxation in the parent country. All profits in all countries that the MNC has affiliates in are subject to tax in their parent's country. Affiliates must pay taxes in their country of residence on the profits earned locally. Local tax payments are deducted from the total tax bill of the MNC. (Otherwise, an affiliate could face over 100 percent taxation). If the tax rate in the parent's country is lower than in that of the affiliate, the affiliate is not subject to additional tax and the "overpayment" may be used to offset tax burden of other affiliates. If the tax rate is higher, the difference must be paid to the parent's home government. However, the difference is only due when the profits are repatriated in the home country. Table 1 shows the tax basis and average rates for the largest investors in the United States. Generally the statutory rates and average rates are similar. The Netherlands have consistently lower tax rates than the statutory rate. There are a number of tax provisions, such as the deductability of royalty income, that allow multinationals to pay much less than the statutory rate on their Dutch investments. (See van Dijk, Weyzig & Murphy (2006) for details on Dutch tax shelters available to multinationals.)

The return data are net of taxes, so ROA should be equalized. However, worldwide taxation can introduce gaps in rates of return that cause the rates of return in the data to deviate from that of the theory. The model predicts that after-tax rates of return are equalized across affiliates:

$$(r_j^{m,i} - \delta_m)(1 - \tau_j - \tau_j^{i,f}) = (r_{j'}^{m,i} - \delta_m)(1 - \tau_{j'} - \tau_{j'}^{i,f}) \qquad (12)$$

They are also equalized between affiliates and with the parent:

$$(r_j^{m,i} - \delta_m)(1 - \tau_i) = (r_j^{m,i} - \delta_m)(1 - \tau_j - \tau_j^{i,f}) \qquad (13)$$

Table 1: Taxation of Multinationals: Average 1990-2001

Country	Tax Basis	Avg. CIT	Data Avg. CIT
Canada	Territorial	35.9	34.4
France	Territorial	36.9	33.7
Germany	Territorial	54.6	34.2
Japan	Worldwide	47.6	50.3
Netherlands	Territorial	35.0	13.4
United Kingdom	Worldwide	32.0	24.8
United States	Worldwide	39.1	39.1

With worldwide taxation, the repatriation taxes are not recorded in the affiliates accounts: $\tau_j^{i,f}$ is not deducted from their profits since the balance of payments is concerned with cross border transactions. Repatriation taxes are payments of domestically owned firms to the home government. Therefore, some of the tax paid on affiliate profits is recorded in the parent's accounts. This shift increases the affiliates' measured return on assets and reduces the parent's returns, since returns are calculated net of taxes. Therefore, we have:

$$(r_i^{m,i} - \delta_m)(1 - \tau_i) - \sum_j [\frac{K_j^{m,i}}{K_i^{m,i}} \tau_j^{i,f}(r_j^{m,i} - \delta_m)] \leq (r_j^{m,i} - \delta_m)(1 - \tau_j) \qquad (14)$$

As shown in Figure 3, the gap between rates paid by U.S. affiliates abroad and the U.S. tax rate has been growing. Corporate tax rates around the world have been falling during this period and investment has shifted to lower tax countries.

4.2 Balanced Growth Path

To examine the effects of multinational taxation on returns, I calculate the balanced growth path equilibrium.

With population growth γ_N, the economy grows at $1 + \gamma_Y = (1 + \gamma_A) * (1 + \gamma_N)$. Per capita income grows at the common productivity trend γ_A. The composition of an

Figure 3: Foreign Corporate Income Tax Rates, 1982-2005

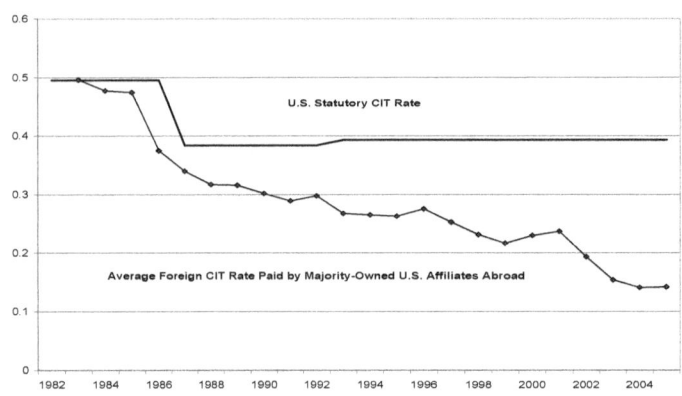

affiliate's asset portfolio is given by:

$$\frac{K_j^{u,i}}{K_j^{m,i}} = \frac{\alpha_u}{\alpha_m}\left(\frac{(\frac{1+\gamma_A}{\beta}-1)(\frac{1}{1-\tau_j-\tau_j^{i,f}})+\delta_m}{\frac{1+\gamma_A}{\beta}-1+\delta_u}\right) \tag{15}$$

Higher taxes shift the affiliate's assets into intangibles. In the steady state, higher corporate taxes lead to higher pre-tax returns as measured by profits over measured capital $\frac{\pi}{K^m}$. When repatriation taxes are not included, this effect induces a measured rate of return gap.

Proposition 4.1. *On the BGP, if country i has worldwide taxation with $\tau_j^{i,f} > 0$ and $\tau_j^j + \tau_j^{i,f} = \tau_i^i$, then $\frac{(1-\tau_j^{i,f}-\tau_j)\pi_j^i}{K_j^{i,m}} > \frac{(1-\tau_i)\pi_i^j}{K_i^{j,m}}$, measured after-tax rate of return of country i's affiliate in territorial taxation country j is higher than j's affiliates in country i.*

Proof. The return on measured assets is given by:

$$\frac{(1-\tau_j-\tau_j^f)\pi_j}{K_j^m} = (1-\tau_j-\tau_j^f)[\frac{1}{\alpha_m}(\frac{\frac{1+\gamma_A}{\beta}-1}{1-\tau-\tau^f}+\delta_m)(\alpha_m+\alpha_u-\alpha_u(\frac{\delta_u+\gamma_Y}{\frac{1+\gamma_A}{\beta}-1+\delta_u}))-\delta_m] \tag{16}$$

14

Table 2: Parameters

α_m	α_u	δ_m	δ_u	τ	β	γ_A	γ_N
0.23	0.1	0.05	0.07	0.39	0.98	0.012	0.01

The tax rate faced by both affiliates is $\tau_j^j + \tau_j^{i,f} = \tau_i^i$ but the $\tau_j^{i,f}$ portion is not measured for country j. Therefore, measured ROA for the worldwide taxing country i is higher:

$$(1 - \tau_i)[\frac{1}{\alpha_m}(\frac{\frac{1+\gamma_A}{\beta} - 1}{1 - \tau_i - \tau_i^{j,f}} + \delta_m)(\alpha_m + \alpha_u - \alpha_u(\frac{\delta_u + \gamma_Y}{\frac{1+\gamma_A}{\beta} - 1 + \delta_u})) - \delta_m] \qquad (17)$$

$\square$

Higher taxes drive up the measured rate of return on tangible assets since there are more unmeasured intangible assets earning returns. Worldwide taxes cause a measured gap since not all affiliates in a country are paying the same tax rate, with territorial tax countries paying the local rate and worldwide tax countries paying their home rate if it is higher. There is a further effect since the Balance of Payments omits the repatriation tax payment.

5 Quantitative Results

This section examines the quantitative effects of different tax treatment. I adjust for the presence of intangible capital and repatriation taxes.

To get a baseline estimate of the effect of taxes on the returns gap, I calibrate the model to estimate intangible capital stocks on the balanced growth path. Capital shares, growth rates and depreciation rates are drawn from McGrattan & Prescott (2008). The tax rate is the average CIT in the United States, including state taxes, from Devereux, Griffith & Klemm (2002). Since U.S. affiliates face repatriation taxes, they are taxed at the domestic rate.

Table 3: Data and Model, 1990-2001

	Data	Model
Inward measured ROA	1.65	4.73
Outward measured ROA	6.37	5.83
Gap	**4.72**	**1.33**

I consolidate FDI across countries to form inward and outward FDI with respect to the United States. Outward investment is subject to repatriation taxes. Over the sample period, U.S. affiliates paid an average of 24.9 percent in corporate income taxes to foreign governments. This implies that the repatriation tax that they face is 14.2 percent.

I do not make any such adjustment for foreign owned affiliates. Most major investor countries use territorial taxation, so are not subject to repatriation taxes. The major investor country with worldwide taxation, the United Kingdom, has a lower tax rate so is also not subject to repatriation taxes on their U.S. investments.

Table 3 compares the model predictions along the balanced growth path for measured rates of returns to the data. Adding intangible capital induces a gap of 1.3 percentage points, about a quarter of the observed gap 4.7 percent.

When these results are applied to the overall asset position, the gap between foreign and U.S. ROA is strongly diminished. Foreigners hold relatively more of their assets in non-FDI assets: FDI assets average 26 percent of inward investment, versus 35 percent for outward. Under the assumption that 1.1 percentage points of the gap is due to the effects of multinational taxation, I reduce U.S. outward FDI ROA by this amount, giving a total of 4.67 for U.S. assets abroad. This reduces the overall gap in the rates of return by a third, from 1.14 to 0.82 percentage points.

In the balanced growth path equilibrium calculated above, after-tax returns are declining in tax rates. Since there are no transaction costs and all countries are the same, rates of return are equalized in the model across countries as well. If there were

Table 4: Adjusting FDI Rates of Return, 1990-2001 (Percent)

	Inward	Outward
$\frac{K^u}{Y}$	0.9	0.7
$\frac{K^m}{Y}$	1.9	1.3
Unadjusted ROA	1.6	6.4
Intangible Adj. ROA	**1.1**	**3.2**
Repatriation & Intan. Adj. ROA	**1.1**	**2.9**

technological differences or differences in cost of funds, rates of return across countries need not be equalized.

While the model generates a gap in returns, it does not match the low returns on inward investment. In the above analysis, I assumed that the economy was on a balanced growth path. The balanced growth path does not capture the low rates of return on inward investment. I discuss reasons for low returns below.

I relax the balanced growth path assumption and parameterize Equation 11 to generate an estimate of the intangible capital-output ratio to expand observed tangible asset holdings. This equality holds in all equilibria, even off the balanced growth path. Tangible capital data are drawn from the BEA's surveys on foreign direct investment. I use value added to measure output Y and net property, plant and equipment plus inventories to measure tangible capital K^m. The rate of return on assets are adjusted using the expression:

$$ROA_{Adj} = ROA \frac{K^m}{Y} \frac{Y}{K^m + K^u} \qquad (18)$$

To account for repatriation taxes, outward ROA is further reduced by the difference between taxes paid abroad and the domestic tax rate: $ROA^{Adj} * (1 - 0.149)$. The results are reported in Table 4.

The gap between the ROA on direct investment abroad and in the United States in reduced from 4.7 to 1.1 percentage points, or three quarters of the gap. Adding intangibles reduces all rates of returns since the observed returns are spread over more assets. However, U.S. returns are reduced more since those firms devote relatively more of their investment to (unmeasured) intangibles while foreign firms invest in (measured) tangible assets. While foreign owned affiliates in the United States and U.S. affiliates abroad have similar R&D expenditures, foreign owned affiliates are much more (tangible) capital intensive.

A higher share of U.S. owned assets abroad are held as FDI (35 percent) than foreign owned assets in the United States (26 percent). Therefore, a larger portion of U.S. returns are adjusted (downward) by including intangible assets in the overall returns on foreign owned assets. In addition, foreign investors receive slightly higher returns on their non-FDI assets than their American counterparts (4.6 versus 4.3 percent). Replacing the rates of return for FDI with the adjusted rates in the overall return on international assets nearly eliminates the gap in returns. The adjusted annual average ROA for foreign owned assets is 3.7 versus 3.8 for U.S. assets abroad, giving a gap of only 0.1 percent. The unadjusted gap is 1.1 percent.

The results provide evidence that intangible assets are a first order source of the FDI returns gap. As shown below, they are robust to a number of checks. However, the estimates are unavoidably imprecise since some of the parameters, such as depreciation of intangible assets, are not directly observable and the methodology does not allow for high frequency estimates. Only estimates of intangible assets based on careful microeconomic data can definitively solve the puzzle.

6 United Kingdom

The United States is not the only country to show a gap in returns. The United Kingdom has a situation very similar to the United States. This section uses the theory to examine this example. The analysis is limited somewhat since the UK does not keep the detailed data on the operations of multinationals that the United States does. However, the available evidence is consistent with multinational taxation being an important part of the explanation of return gap.

As can be seen in Figure 4, since 1997 the United Kingdom developed a situation

Figure 4: Foreign-Owned Assets in U.K. BOP, 1976-2004

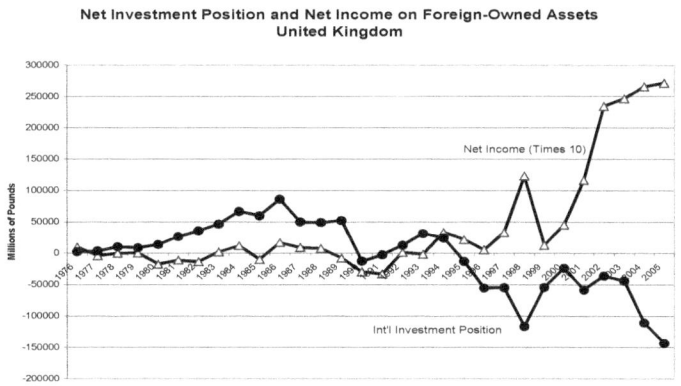

Net Investment Position and Net Income on Foreign-Owned Assets
United Kingdom

similar to the U.S. case: positive earnings on a negative international investment position. Like the United States, the positive earnings despite a negative international investment position is due to a gap in ROA, specifically in FDI assets (Figure 5)[2]. The imbalances have been less pronounced in the UK than in the United States, but have been growing recently. The average overall gap in returns from 1997 to 2005 was 0.53 percentage points.

The United Kingdom taxes MNCs using worldwide taxation. Since the UK does not keep data on the balance sheets of its foreign affiliates, we do not know what repatriation taxes, if any, British MNCs face. As an estimate of the taxes they face, I weight the tax rate paid by U.S. affiliates by UK FDI assets for countries that are major destinations for British investment[3]. I use statutory rate from Devereux et al. (2002) for the U.S. rate. As can be seen from Figure 6, UK MNCs faced repatriation taxes over most

---

[2]Unlike the United States, which reports current cost estimates, the UK data only values FDI assets at book value.

[3]The countries are Canada, France, Germany, Ireland, Japan, the Netherlands and the United States. These countries account for about 70 percent of British foreign direct investment assets abroad. Unlike the U.S. case, FDI assets are valued at book value.

Figure 5: U.K. Returns to Foreign Investment, 1979-2004 (Percent)

(a) FDI returns

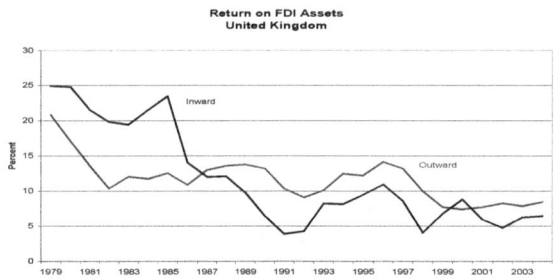

(b) Non-FDI Returns

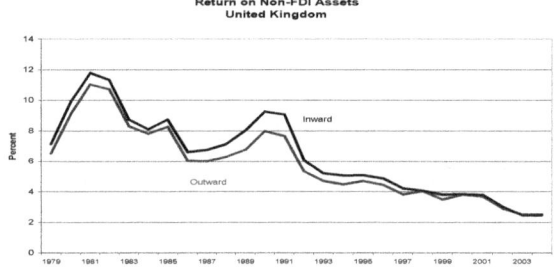

of the period[4]. In fact, the data may overstate the tax paid abroad, since it excludes a number of tax havens, such as Bermuda, that have sizable British investment. Further, the British MNCs have a higher share of investment in the Netherlands than U.S. MNCs, increasing the scope for reducing profits in other countries using Dutch tax shelters.

As a baseline, I examine the period from 1997 to 2005, the period in which the UK runs a negative IIP. The returns gap begins in 1987. The late 1980s were of period

---

[4]Annual international investment position data by country is only available for the UK starting in 1987.

Figure 6: UK Tax Rates, 1984-2005

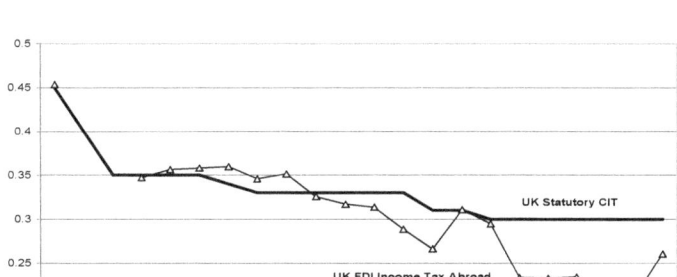

of significant change in taxes as a result of the Thatcher reforms in the UK and the 1986 tax reform in the United States, the most important destination for British investment. It is not clear what expectations managers at MNCs had about the tax burden they would be facing, especially since investment begins to shift from higher tax countries like France to the low tax destinations like the Netherlands and Ireland. Examining the later period avoids changes in MNC investments that may have accompanied these reforms.

I use the rate of return equalization method rather than calculating the balance growth path since both inward and outward FDI grew rapidly during this period, suggesting that the UK was not on a balanced growth path.

The UK does not collect the data required to do the same adjustments as were done for the United States. As a rough estimate, I adjust the UK rates of return using the average statutory corporate income tax for the UK (0.302) and the estimated tax faced by British affiliates abroad (0.250) for 1997 to 2005. The technology parameters are the same as those used in the U.S. calculation and I use the tangible capital/value added ratio for all British non-financial private corporations from the Blue Book for both inward and outward investment (from the perspective of UK).

21

Table 5: Adjusting UK FDI Rates of Return, 1997-2005 (Percent)

	Inward	Outward
$\frac{K^u}{Y}$	0.9	0.9
$\frac{K^m}{Y}$	2.0	2.0
Unadjusted ROA	6.70	9.26
Intangible Adj. ROA	**4.67**	**6.46**
Repatriation & Intan. Adj. ROA	**4.67**	**6.12**

The results are reported in Table 5. Intangibles close almost half of the gap, dropping it from 2.56 to 1.45 percentage points. This result is robust to different time periods. Expanding the time period to 1987 to 2005 (the entire period that the UK shows a gap) gives similar results. The adjustments reduce the gap from 3.15 to 1.93 percentage points, 40 percent of the gap.

Replacing the adjusted rates of return on FDI in the overall rates of return on foreign owned assets from 1997 to 2005 reducing the gap by half, from 0.53 to 0.26 percentage points. (3.76 percent on outward versus 3.5 percent on inward investment). FDI investment is less important in the UK, both outward (17.4 percent of assets) and inward (10 percent), so the large gap in FDI assets are muted compared to the U.S. case.

While this calculation is necessarily rough, there is additional evidence that intangibles are an important part of the gap. Nickell (2006) has argued that the gap can be explained by the undervaluation of FDI assets, which are valued at book value. Pratten (1996) estimates the estimates the 1991 ratio of market value to book value of British FDI assets abroad and foreign owned assets in the UK to be 1.75 and 1.50 respectively. Kubelec, Orskaug & Tanaka (2007) updates this estimate for 2005 using stock market index changes to obtain 2.05 and 1.65. The higher value of British assets abroad is enough to flip the net international investment position from negative to positive.

As further evidence, it is notable that R&D expenditures as a share of GDP fell during the 1980s, from 1.9 percent in 1981 to 1.5 percent in the mid-1990s, suggesting that expenditures on intangibles fell after corporate taxes were cut.

7 Discussion

This section discusses the validity of the underlying assumptions and the results.

The methodology does not allow for high frequency estimates of intangibles and exclude intangible capital obtained from parents and sister affiliates in other countries. The adjustments use parameter values that are not directly observable to measure assets that are not currently measured. Therefore, they are subject to error. This section presents some checks on the results to see if they are consistent with other data and parameter values. I find that the results hold up under a number of robustness checks.

7.1 Openness

In the model all intangible investment is done locally. For some types of intangibles, this assumption is not very strong. It is unlikely that much of the organization capital identified by Prescott & Visscher (1980), such as job-employee matches and firm specific human capital, is likely the result of investment done outside that affiliate. However, some intangibles (what McGrattan & Prescott (2008) refer to as "technology capital"), such as process innovations, may flow between countries. Unlike physical assets, whose location can easily be determined, intangibles may move within a firm without leaving a trail (Lipsey 2008).

Intangible capital mobility likely strengthens the results. MNCs based in countries with territorial taxation have an incentive to expense their intangible investment in countries with high taxes since it reduces measured profits. Countries with worldwide taxation have less incentive to do so since the tax burden is determined by the MNC's total profits. Shifting profits across does not reduce the tax burden when they are repatriated. Relatively high taxes gives inward investors an incentive to do their intangible investment in their U.S. affiliates, lowering measured U.S. returns. Therefore, high tax locations will appear to have abnormally low returns. The model is a lower bound on the effects of taxes since it does not include this effect.

There is evidence that MNCs perform R&D in the United States for export to other countries. Griffith, Harrison & Reenen (2004) find that U.S. R&D spending flows to British firms if the British firm has a presence in the United States. The United States runs a surplus in royalty payments (Robbins 2006).

McGrattan & Prescott (2008) argue that historically the United States has been relatively closed to foreign investment until the 1970s. Indeed, there have been substantial capital flows into the United States since then. During a transition to a new steady state brought about by opening to foreign capital, foreign-owned assets in the United States may yield low measured returns since investment in intangibles will be higher than in the steady state. Since this investment is expensed, measured returns will be reduced. Part of the lower return is young firms building up organization capital (Mataloni 2000). (For a model of this process, see Atkeson & Kehoe (2005).) This factor very well may be an important part of the solution. Tax differentials do not completely close the gap, nor does the openness. A combination of both may more fully explain the difference.

7.2 Robustness

As a robustness check, I re-estimate U.S. inward and outward foreign intangible capital using a procedure from McGrattan & Prescott (2005). They estimate intangible capital stock for the United States using a growth accounting framework and then estimate another country's intangible capital stocks by assuming that the ratio of the intangible capital-output ratio and R&D expenditure share of output across economies are the same across economies. An advantage of this approach is that we do not need to take a stand on the depreciation rate on intangible capital.

Let RD_j be research and development expenditures. Intangible assets are calculated by comparing affiliate R&D expenditures with those of a reference economy, in this case the U.S. private business sector.

$$\frac{K_j^u}{Y_j} = \frac{K_{US}^u}{Y_{US}} \frac{RD_j}{Y_j} \frac{Y_{US}}{RD_{US}} \tag{19}$$

Table 6 presents the results of this alternative approach. The results are robust to using this method. The results are very similar to the non-balanced growth path estimates of U.S. FDI returns (Table 4). The alternative inward and outward adjusted FDI rates of return are 0.9 and 3.1 percent respectively versus 1.1 and 2.9 percent. The similarity of the gap is remarkable given that the alternative estimates use a different

Table 6: Alternative Adjustment to U.S. Rates of Return, 1990-2001 (Percent)

	U.S. Bus. Sector	Inward	Outward
$\frac{RD}{Y}$	2.1	5.5	3.2
$\frac{K^m}{Y}$	1	1.9	1.3
$\frac{K^u}{Y}$	0.65	0.88	0.68
Unadjusted ROA	4.1	1.6	6.4
Intangible Adj. ROA	**2.4**	**0.9**	**3.6**
Repatriation + Intang. Adj. ROA	**2.4**	**0.9**	**3.1**

methodology and independent data.

7.3 Taxes

Implementing taxes in the model raises a number of difficulties. While they are represented by a single rate in the model, in reality the corporate tax code is extremely complex. While corporate income taxes are generally not progressive, a major issue is calculating personal income taxes, there are a number of complexities. Different industries may be subject to different tax rates. FDI investments may get tax breaks to encourage the selection of a particular area for investment. The use of tax havens and financial engineering may trim tax burdens. Backus, Henriksen & Storesletten (2008) note that statutory rates do not appear to match very well with actual tax payments or investment behavior.

Worldwide taxation introduces additional complexity to the taxes faced by MNCs. Foreign-owned affiliates under territorial taxes largely face the same incentives as domestic firms since they are taxed the same way. Since worldwide taxation can induce repatriation tax liabilities, there may be an incentive to retain earnings strategically (Hines 1999, Desai, Foley & Hines 2001). Kozlow & Abaroa (2006) argue that MNC behavior in response to the American Jobs Creation Act (AJCA) shows that such strategic behavior is important. Given that such strategic behavior, it is not clear that repatriation taxes should be counted by their full value. The theoretical literature has not developed a consensus. (For example, see Altshuler, Newlon & Randolph (1995) and Altshuler & Grubert (2002).)

It is notable that MNCs appear to be equalizing rates of return according to statutory rates. The average after-tax ROA for U.S. Parents from 1993 to 2001 was 2.9 percent. The pre-tax ROA for Majority-Owned Foreign Affiliates (MOFAs) over that period was 5.1 percent. The implied tax rate on MOFA's profits to set the two rates equal is 43.1 percent, not far from the statutory rate of 39.1 percent. Since affiliates only recorded a tax rate of 24.9 percent, the actual ROA is 3.9 percent. The data are consistent with MNC's equalizing rates of return subject to the home tax rate.

Even if repatriation taxes do not reduce returns by the full amount, the inclusion of intangible assets alone closes the gap a great deal. The fact that affiliates under worldwide taxes hold more retained earnings suggests that repatriation taxes do bind MNC's behavior at least to some degree. The reaction to the AJCA shows that MNC's behavior is not neutral to taxes. Therefore, it is reasonable that different tax systems induce different investment portfolios. Investing in intangible assets provides a partial way around corporate income taxes, which may be used even if financial engineering can be used to reduce the repatriation tax burden.

8 Conclusion

This paper estimates aggregate intangible capital stocks for foreign owned affiliates and suggest a significant role for different holdings of intangible assets due to corporate income taxes. Adjusting rates of return for intangible assets reduces the U.S. FDI returns gap from 4.7 to 1.1 percentage points over the period 1990 to 2001, accounting for about three quarters of the gap. Similar adjustments reduce the British FDI returns gap by 40 percent.

While the results are consistent with intangible assets being an important source of the gap, other factors may account for it. Indeed, the analysis does not account for the full gap indicating that additional factors are at work. A full accounting of the true impact of intangibles will require a careful micro level estimate of these assets.

A Data Appendix

Table 1

- Average Statutory Corporate Income Tax: Devereux et al. (2002).

- Average Empirical Corporate Income Tax: U.S.: NIPA Table 6.17B. Corporate Profits Before Tax by Industry. Other Countries: USDIA Table III.E.1.

Table 4

- Return on Assets: Payments to direct investment divided by direct investment assets with market value adjustment.

- $\frac{RD}{Y}$: R&D performed by affiliates divided by value added.

- $\frac{K^M}{Y}$: Net gross property, plant and equipment plus inventories divided by value added.

Figure 1

- Assets: International Investment Position, Table 1, Line 1.

- Net Income: Balance of Payments, Table 1, lines 12 and 29.

Figure 2

- FDI Assets: International Investment Position, FDI assets with market pricing adjustment.

- Non-FDI Assets: Total non-financial derivatives assets less FDI.

- Net Income: Balance of Payments, Table 1, lines 12 and 29 less income to FDI.

Figure 3

- Statutory Corporate Income Tax: Devereux et al. (2002).

- Affiliate tax rate: Foreign corporate income tax paid over pre-tax net income, majority owned foreign affiliates.

Figure 4

- IIP: Foreign Direct Investment (Release MA4), U.K. National Statistics Office.

- Net Income: U.K. National Statistics Office, series HJYW-HJYX.

Figure 5

- ROA: U.K. National Statistics Office, series HBOH, HBOI.

References

Altshuler, Rosanne & Harry Grubert (2002), 'Repatriation taxes, repatriation strategies and multinational financial policy', *Journal of Public Economics* **87**(1), 73–107.

Altshuler, Rosanne, T. Scott Newlon & William C. Randolph (1995), Do repatriation taxes matter?: Evidence from the tax returns of U.S. multinationals, *in* M.Feldstein, J.Hines & G.Hubbard, eds, 'The Effects of International Taxation on Multinational Corporations', University of Chicago Press, Chicago, pp. 253–272.

Atkeson, Andrew & Patrick Kehoe (2005), 'Modeling and measuring organization capital', *Journal of Political Economy* **113**(5), 1026–1053.

Backus, David, Espen Henriksen & Kjetil Storesletten (2008), 'Taxes and the global allocation of capital', *Journal of Monetary Economics* **55**(1), 48–61.

Bernard, Andrew, J. Bradford Jensen & Peter Schott (2006), Transfer pricing by U.S. based multinational firms, Manuscript, Tuck School of Business, Dartmouth University.

Caballero, Ricardo J., Emmanuel Farhi & Pierre-Olivier Gourinchas (2008), 'An equilibrium model of 'global imbalances' and low interest rates', *American Economic Review* **98**(1), 358–393.

Carson, Carol S., Bruce T. Grimm & Carol E. Moylan (1994), 'A satellite account for research and development', *Survey of Current Business* pp. 37–71.

Curcuru, Stephanie, Tomas Dvorak & Francis Warnock (2008), 'Cross-border returns differentials', *Quarterly Journal of Economics* .

Desai, Mihir A., C. Fritz Foley & James R. Hines (2001), 'Repatriation taxes and dividend distortions', *National Tax Journal* **54**(4), 829–851.

Devereux, Michael P., Rachel Griffith & Alexander Klemm (2002), 'Corporate income tax reforms and international tax competition', *Economic Policy* **17**(35), 451–495.

Doms, Mark & J. Bradford Jensen (1998), Comparing wages, skills, and productivity between domestically owned and foreign-owned manufacturing establishments in the united states, *in* R. E.Baldwin, R. E.Lipsey & J. D.Richardson, eds, 'Geography and Ownership as Bases of Economic Accounting', University of Chicago Press, Chicago, pp. 235–255.

Forbes, Kristen (2008), Why do foreigners invest in the United States?, Discussion Paper 13908, NBER.

Girma, Sourafel, Steve Thompson & Peter W. Wright (2002), 'Why are productivity and wages higher in foreign firms', *Economic and Social Review* **33**(1), 93–100.

Gourinchas, Pierre-Olivier & Helene Rey (2006), From world banker to world venture capitalist: The US external adjustment and the exorbitant privilege, *in* R.Clarida, ed., 'G7 Current Account Imbalances: Sustainability and Adjustment', University of Chicago Press, Chicago, pp. 11–55.

Griffith, Rachel, Rupert Harrison & John Van Reenen (2004), How special is the special relationship?: Using the impact of U.S. R&D spillovers as a test of technology sourcing, Discussion Paper 4698, CEPR.

29

Hausmann, Ricardo & Frederico Sturzenegger (2007), 'The missing dark matter in the wealth of nations and its implications for global imbalances', *Economic Policy* **22**(51), 469 – 518.

Hines, James R. (1999), 'Lessons from behavioral responses to international taxation', *National Tax Journal* **52**(2), 305–322.

Hung, Juann H. & Angelo Mascaro (2004), Return on cross-border investment: Why does U.S. investment abroad do better?, Technical Paper 2004-17, Congressional Budget Office.

Kapicka, Marek (2008), How important is technology capital?: Measurement and theory, mimeo, UCSB.

Kozlow, Ralph & Patricia Abaroa (2006), U.S. multinational companies, dividends, and taxes, mimeo, Bureau of Economic Analysis.

Kubelec, Chris, Bjorn-Erik Orskaug & Misa Tanaka (2007), 'Financial globalization, external balance sheets and economic adjustment', *Bank of England Quarterly Bulletin* **47**(2), 244–257.

Landefeld, J. Steven, Ann M. Lawson & Douglas B. Weinberg (1992), 'Rates of return on direct investment', *Survey of Current Business* pp. 79–86.

Laster, David S. & Robert N. McCauley (1994), 'Making sense of the profits of foreign firms in the United States', *FRBNY Quarterly Review* pp. 44–75.

Lev, Baruch & Theodore Sougiannis (1996), 'The capitalization, amortization, and value-relevance of R&D', *Journal of Accounting and Economics* **21**(1), 107–138.

Lipsey, Robert E. (2008), Measuring the location of production in a world of intangible productive assets, FDI, and intrafirm trade, Working Paper 14121, NBER.

Mataloni, Raymond (2000), 'An examination of the low rates of return of foreign-owned U.S. companies', *Survey of Current Business* pp. 55–73.

McGrattan, Ellen & Edward C. Prescott (2005), 'Taxes, regulations, and the value of U.S. and U.K. corporations', *Review of Economic Studies* **72**(3), 767–796.

McGrattan, Ellen & Edward C. Prescott (2008), Technology capital and the U.S. current account, Staff Report 406, Federal Reserve Bank of Minneapolis.

Meissner, Christopher M. & Alan M. Taylor (2006), Losing our marbles in the new century?: The great rebalancing in historical perspective, Working Paper 12580, NBER.

Mendoza, Enrique, Vincenzo Quadrini & Victor Rios-Rull (2007), Financial integration, financial deepness and global imbalances, mimeo, University of Minnesota.

Nickell, Stephen (2006), 'The UK current account deficit and all that', *Bank of England Quarterly Bulletin* **46**(2), 231–239.

Okubo, Sumiye, Carol A. Robbins, Carol E. Moylan, Brian K. Sliker, Laura I. Schultz & Lisa S. Mataloni (2006), R&D satellite account: Preliminary estimates, mimeo, Bureau of Economic Analysis and National Science Foundation.

Pratten, Cliff (1996), *The Valuation of Outward and Inward Direct Investment*, Cambridge University.

Prescott, Edward C. & M. Visscher (1980), 'Organization capital', *Journal of Political Economy* **88**(3), 446–461.

Robbins, Carol (2006), Measuring payments for the supply and use of intellectual property, mimeo, Bureau of Economic Analysis.

U.S. Deparment of the Treasury Internal Revenue Service (1999), Measuring payments for the supply and use of intellectual property, Publication 3218 (4-1999).

van Dijk, Michiel, Francis Weyzig & Richard Murphy (2006), The Netherlands: A tax haven?, Technical report, SOMO (Centre for Research on Multinational Corporations).

World Bank (2006), *Where is the Wealth of Nations?: Measuring Capital for the 21st Century*, World Bank, Washington.